U0045137

í

AM

BORN

TO

WRITE

in THE Name OF LOVE

CARMEN LEI

PREFACE

THE LINGUIST H. G. WIDDOWSON ONCE SAID PROVOCATIVELY THAT THE VALUE OF POETRY LIES IN ITS VERY USELESSNESS. ALTHOUGH POETRY SERVES NO PRACTICAL PURPOSE, IT HAS GREAT VALUE. POETRY IS THE MEANS BY WHICH WE EXPRESS OUR DEEPEST FEELINGS AND MOST UNIQUE INSIGHTS. POETRY IS THE LANGUAGE OF THE SOUL.

ONE ENGAGES IN THE ACT OF WRITING POETRY FOR ALL SORTS OF REASONS BUT NEVER, I AM CONVINCED, FOR PROFIT. ONE WRITES BECAUSE ONE HAS SOMETHING TO SAY, IMPELLED BY SOME INTUITION OR EMOTION TO FASHION OUT OF ORDINARY LANGUAGE A UNIQUE AND PERSONAL VERBAL ARTEFACT.

THE POEMS IN THIS COLLECTION ARE A LABOUR OF LOVE. THEY WERE WRITTEN FOR NO OTHER PURPOSE THAN TO ARTICULATE A PARTICULAR VIEW OF LIFE. TOGETHER THESE POEMS EXPRESS A POIGNANT AND PENETRATING CONSCIOUSNESS ENGAGING WITH THE WORLD THAT WE ALL SHARE. IN THESE PAGES, THE MUNDANE FABRIC OF EVERYDAY LIFE IS RENDERED IN FRESH AND DELIGHTFUL VIGNETTES. EVERY SYLLABLE RADIATES PURE ENJOYMENT OF LIFE. THE LITTLE TIPPLER IS, OH SO CLEARLY HERE, LEANING AGAINST THE SUN.

THERE IS A COMMON TENDENCY TO SEEK ENLIGHTENMENT AND MEANING IN POETRY. SUCH AN URGE, IN MY VIEW, SHOULD BE RESISTED. A POEM SHOULD BE ENJOYED ORGANICALLY. THE CADENCE OF THE LINES, THE ARRANGEMENT OF SYLLABLES ARE ASSEMBLED IN A UNIQUE ORDER THAT FUSES WITH THE SEMANTICS OF THE COLLOCATIONS. A POEM IS A GLOBED FRUIT, AS ARCHIBALD MACLEISH SAYS. ENJOY IT WHOLE.

PROF. CHIU MAN YIN,

DEPARTMENT OF ENGLISH,
UNIVERSITY OF MACAU.

PREFACE

JUST LIKE HER PAINTINGS, LEI KA MAN'S POEMS POP. HER WORDS EXPLODE LIKE FIREWORKS, SPARKLE LIKE STARDUST, AND FINALLY TOUCH YOUR HEART. HER POEMS ARE A WINDOW THAT TAKES YOU TO HER WORLD, A WORLD FILLED WITH SENTIMENTS, ADVENTURES, AND SURPRISES. IN THIS WORLD, YOU SOMETIMES SMILE, BUT YOU ALSO SOMETIMES CRY. KA MAN'S WORLD IS NOT ONLY MADE UP OF WORDS, BUT ALSO POWERFUL COLORS AND TEXTURES, AS WELL AS IMAGINATION AND DREAMS. READING KA MAN'S POEMS ALWAYS MAKES ME FEEL LIKE I AM TALKING WITH HER. HER USE OF (I, YOU, WE) IS HOW SHE CONVERSES WITH HER READERS. I APPRECIATE HOW KA MAN'S COLLECTION IS FULL OF CONTRADICTIONS ABOUT LIFE BECAUSE AS MOST OF US CAN RELATE - LIFE IS ALLURING BECAUSE IT CAN SOMETIMES GET CONTRADICTORY. WE MAY ALL EXPERIENCE AND INTERPRET KA MAN'S WORLD DIFFERENTLY, AND I CANNOT WAIT FOR YOU TO JOIN ME ON THIS WONDERFUL RIDE.

MIRANDA SIN I MA

PRESIDENT, MACAO ASSOCIATION FOR THE ADVANCEMENT OF
ENGLISH LANGUAGE TEACHING
SENIOR INSTRUCTOR, UNIVERSITY OF MACAU

IN THE NAME OF LOVE
THE FIRST NAME :

Mania

Lies 18

Let Me 19

Cutters & Sawblades 20

I Wish I Could 21

A Jar Of Heart 22

Bury 23

Membrane 24

The Rusty Book 25

Frustration 26

Dribs & Drabs 27

Pain 28

The Coin 29

The Long Escape 30

Our Song 31

Enough 32

Ribbon 33

Devil 34

Haunted 35

Secret 36

The Love You Give 37

The 14th Chapter 38

Trash 39

Split 40

Empty 41

The Mountaintop 42

Here To 43

I Fight 44

In Vain 45

The Weapon 46

Kill-time Therapy 47

Cry A Little 48

Odd 49

Only If 50

Scrawl 51

All Alone 52

Into The Night 53

Very Much On Time 54

The Withered Rose 55

She 56

Falling 57

Maybe Not 58

Screw 59

It Hurts 60

The Solution 61

Sin 62

Here & There 63

Tears Of Nowhere 64

Toss & Turn 65

Falling Steps 66

The Forlorn Cold 67

The Lone Air 68

The End 69

IN THE NAME OF LOVE
THE MIDDLE NAME :

Eros

Once   74

Fragrance   75

I Think Of You   76

Morning Blue   77

Insomnia   78

Rain   79

Longing For   80

The East & The West   81

Kotor Heart   82

Road Trip   83

The Blood Moon   84

More Than December   85

Fill Me   86

The Ferris Wheel   87

Give You Poetry   88

So Poetry   89

Right   90

The Wrong Hug   91

Mosaic   92

Perfect Pitch   93

Breath   96

More & More   97

98	Lost
99	A Crying Shadow
100	Under The Shade
101	Secretly In Love
102	A Love Letter
103	Good Night
104	Drug
105	Upside Down
106	Quit
107	Press Against
108	Kisses
109	Scent
110	Touch
111	Blueprint
112	Linger
113	Will You (Verse I)
114	Will You (Verse II)
115	Will You (Verse III)
116	The Manifest
117	The Figment
118	The Haunting Night
119	A Lifetime A Day

IN THE NAME OF LOVE
THE LAST NAME :

PRAGMA

●   ●

// YOU ARE THE REASON
I WRITE //

127

// YOU ARE THE REASON
I FALL //
– ALL IN OR NOTHING

128

// YOU ARE THE REASON
I AWAIT //

129

// YOU ARE THE REASON
I DARE //

130

// YOU ARE THE REASON
I GLITTER //
– GIVE YOU A SUNSET

131

// YOU ARE THE REASON
I CHERISH //

132

// YOU ARE THE REASON
I RISE //

133

●   ●

// YOU ARE THE REASON
I DROWN //

134

// YOU ARE THE REASON
I SEEK //

135

I WILL KNOW YOU
ONCE AGAIN

136

TIMING KNOWS NO LOVE

137

KEEP WAITING

138

DON'T WANT YOU
TO SEE ME WEEP

139

IN THE ENDS
OF THE EARTH

140

in the name of love in the name of love in the name of love in the name of love in the name of love in the name of love in the name of love in the name of love in the name of love in the name of love in the name of love in the name of love in the name of love in the name of

name of love in the name of love in the

THE FIRST NAME :

Mania

Lies

Your lies are revealed from a lava kiss
that burns me into the darkness of your soul;
I am alone with your healing hug and smile
When all of a sudden I see your back
Hiding from me and holding his rescue.
From then I know I am unloved with
All your words, your smiles and your lies.

Let Me

Let me buy you roses,
Though he gives you bruises;
Let me give you comfort,
Though he gives no effort;
Let me count you petals,
Though you follow his shadows;
Let me count your wrinkles,
Though he is not that ethical;
Let me read you a book,
Though you want his look;
Let me bring you stars,
Though he gives you scars;
Let me love one like love thee,
Though you don't want me.

Cutters & Sawblades

You paved me with stones,
With cutters all around and
Yucky sawblades scatter around.

I Wish I Could

I wish I could
Forget all broken memories you give me

I wish I could
Forget all the pleasant pains you give me

I wish I could
Bear all the mournful loneliness he gives you

I wish I could forget
But not the sinful innocence of your face

A Jar Of Heart

You broke my heart into fragments;
she came to me and picked those
and put them in a jar of heart.
She mended it and put together
an imperfect yet intact heart.

Bury

I put a seed into your heart, and a
Dandelion grows within. Nothing
Can mar its beauty or ruin its bloom.
Peculiarly allergic to your pollen, I
Find myself awfully sensitive to your
Deadly skin. I dare not touch it, I
Dare not to. I know, even if I try, it
Will be destroyed with just a gentle
Touch. Now, I will bury the seed instead.

Membrane

You hold the wrapped leaves
On one hand with aged filler.
Your forefinger deadly swirls
The cigar on bitter rainy day.
Exhaling a mouthful of tepid
Nutty smoke in the oaken air
You smell the nicotine which
Goes right into blood stream.
Your kissable lips light up my
Heart like a hungry vampire.
I taste your every vapor-like
Breath and inhale down into
My lungs to my vessels and
Breathe out into membranes
Of your dry and spicy mouth.

The Rusty Book

I read your poetic heart
And I study every single
Line of it to find out
That it is torn into pieces
Just like my rusty book
On my abandoned shelf
Without anyone reading
It but I will fix it until it is
Completed in my hand.

Frustration

You are a book
Which I start with excitement
But I finish reading it
With frustration

Dribs &
Drabs

I beg you, I beg you
For a mere rescue
From the dribs and drabs

Pain

Pain is

Losing your own dignity
Crying your heart out
Searching your own identity
Revealing your inner secrets
Forcing to be assimilated
Showing a mask to others
Finding difficult to trust
Saying a forever goodbye
Seeing you leave

The Coin

You toss a coin
Into the pond

Left or right
Right or wrong

Let it decide
Fate or plan

You don't know
Should let her go

While I pray and
Make a wish

I was the coin
You never let go

The Long Escape

I took a long flight
To somewhere I
Don't belong to.
I took a long break
To somewhere I
Don't crave for.
I took a long escape
From your heart which
I don't attach to.

Our Song

You sang that song
Casually with a smile.
Shyly did I sing along
Consciously in heart.
The silly me took that
Seriously as I
Called it our song.

Enough

Too many different stories at one time
Too many people suffering at the same time

You and I have created enough stories
To make each other suffer for a long time

Ribbon

I put a ribbon round your neck
And I pull it close to me
Closer and closer it comes
Until you push me away
Like a helpless child
Who wants to get rid of a ghost

Devil

the
devil
in
me
loves
the
angel
in
you

Haunted

I am haunted; I have swirled
into a hole where the dark
and the devil reside. I want
to survive all alone and listen
to the silent heartbeat where
the ulterior pain stays loudly.
I yelled out your name once.
Your intangible touch left me
scars in the hole. I feel the urge
to leave but I just cannot move.
I keep falling into your trap until
swirls of ashes come out from
the heavenly indescribable hole.

Secret

If you can tell my stories
Through my eyes
Please do not say
It out loud

If you can see my scars
Through my heart
Please do not say
It out loud

Because these are my
Last dignity to my soul
And this is a secret
Only we two know

The Love You Give

The love you give is

Beautifully torn
Preciously lost
Entirely broken
Perfectly wrong
Kindly sinful
　Gently painful
　　Warmly bitter

　　Yet
　　　It is still softly loud
　　　In my heart

The 14th Chapter

What if I told you on that night
That I would like to be the light
Which lightened your sky bright

What if I told you on that night
That I would like to hold you tight
In my arms to make you feel alright

What if I told you on that night
But now I don't even have the right
To turn back the clock to that night

Trash

Thinking of you like
I'm literal trash

Memories fading like
They're literal ash

Split

The relationship split
When distance cracked
In between the boundaries
Within two abnormal hearts
Find uncertainties and want to
Take the fall and to risk it all to love.

Empty

You will find me empty

But with you lie within.

The Mountaintop

I stand on a mountaintop;
Sometimes it is quite a scramble
To feel the lonesome wind
When it is dull and cloudy.

I stand on a mountaintop;
Sometimes it is quite a comfort
To feel the deserted mist
When it is dusky and gloomy.

I stand on a mountaintop;
Sometimes it is quite a pain
To feel the silence of solitude
When you are too far to reach.

Here To

I scattered
I broke
Still
I am here to fix

I shallowed
I dismantled
Still
I am here to mend

I drowned
I yelled
Still
You are not here to heal

I Fight

I fight to
Leach out
Your mole
On my hand

I fight to
Grub up
Your blemish
On my skin

I fight until
I realise I
Was only
Once In you

In Vain

I wish upon a star
To want to know where you are
I fumbled my way through the crowd
Sniffing your scent in a shroud

Away behind me a bluish mist
There I was freezing in the midst
Calling your first name all in vain
It turned to vapour with pain and rain

Hardly could I remember your warmth
When you left me alone in the north
Three feet deep on the rose of snow
I lost you and finally I came to know

The Weapon

To make me suffer
You know how
You know well

Step by step
You know how
You know well

How you kill
How you break
I know well

Kill-time Therapy

It is a tragedy if I make you my priority
But you take me as your kill-time therapy

Cry A Little

I cry a little
Cry to feel
Cry to heal

Tears become illiterate
When they mask the twist
Darkness wants to play
They drop on my knees
They freeze on my toes
And I swallow a hard dose

Taking the blame is truly a shame
But crying is not the same
When I know the crystal drops
Are the gifts of God
Covering the dust at dusk
Blinding the evil in people

I know I can cry a little
But not too hard
But not too strong
At least
At the moment
I cry a little

Odd

It's quite odd to break and mend
At the same time
It's quite odd to collapse and rise
At the same time
But it's not odd to hate and love
At the same time
When I sweat your sweat
When I ache your ache
It's odd to accept what's offered
As your life descends into chaos
You are a lost thing in you
 I have once touched your bruises
  I have once called your name
   I know
     You're somebody to me
      But I'm nobody to you

Only If

If I were to love you
You would send me roses of thorns
You would give me hugs of guilt.
Only if I were to love you
But I chose not to
And so did you

Scrawl

I scrawl a butterfly
I scrawl it on my own
I scrawl it in your eye
Until your bone is shown
I wait for another July
When I sit here on my own
To make my scrawl known

All Alone

I like the way you ignore me
I like the way you scorn me
I like to hide in the corner
Dancing on my own
Seeing you under the light
When I stand here all alone
I hate the way you please me
I hate the way you call me
I hate to hide in that corner
Dancing on my own
Seeing you kiss her
When I stand here all alone

Into
The Night

My eyelids fell into the night
I did enjoy the fall out of nothing at all
I have never got the rescue right
And I stretched to make a subtle haul

My eyelids fell into the night
I kept in touch with the toxic fall
Until I was given a weighty bite
And I oppressed your somber call

I poured myself into the night
When I expected a silent downfall
As you sent me an obvious slight
And I couldn't love you anymore

Very Much On Time

You are very much on time
Before I take it for granted
And before you give it a go

You are very much on time
After I spent those lonely nights
And after you shared the alcohols

You are very much on time
When I was already lost
And you were just that on time

The Withered Rose

The withered rose in the ice
Speaks truth to its thorns:
The sharp prickles stab
Into the cold and the dark
Celebration is still too early
For the rose to bloom
Its thorns connect memories
Between the past and present
It cannot wait for another winter
As the ice melts into the petals
Anyone in the wood picks it up
Before another Christmas comes
It does not want to admit that
It is going to die tonight
After it is stepped on by blight

She

She has a fragile smile which I have to take care of.
She talks with lies and gives it a try.
I cannot stand seeing her in the cold
and I touch her with a trembling finger uncontrolled.
I push myself harder to reach her, until the street lights
and the pedestrians get blurred.

She used to hold a handbag with a brand,
her eyeglasses reflected me unplanned.
With a shame, I secretly look at her name
and my eyes follow all her way day by day.
Let me be in the dark without a spark for
she does not want to understand me more.

Falling

Don't make me love you
With your aloof smile
Don't approach me
Don't talk to me
As I can't control
To fall for you
Don't make me love you
And turn your back and
Run away for you are
Afraid that you will
Fall for me too

Maybe Not

Your smile is worth my thousand thoughts
No one can tell how, no one can tell why
I try to capture every part of you
Bit by bit, little by little
You and I, maybe not
Our story is as brief as a song
Just as ridiculous when we look at each other
Sometimes, we exchange dreams at night
When the whole world falls asleep
No one is creeping, no one is talking
Too many feelings and too much silence
For my mind is filled with your existence
You and I, maybe not
May not be

Screw

I want to fix my heart
When I know
The only way to heal
Is to hide it
From you;
Maybe not,
Not to fix it
But to screw it,
Instead.

It Hurts

Whenever I drown for you
It hurts

The umbrella stands still
When the rain pours and roars
I wait at the corner
Humming the songs you sang before
The acid erodes the memories in my head
That really hurts

I turn my back looking for someone like you
Whenever I drown for you
It rains
And it hurts

The Solution

When my throat
Clogs up with your name
When my arms are
Embarrassingly hard
I'll quit
In silence
Your tears linger
In my head sometimes
I'll wait until
They have become mist
I'll wait until I
No longer want them

Sin

the lighter
ignites
the sin
the guilt
the evil
but the sinner feels like in heaven
when she takes the blame
and tastes the forbidden pleasure

Here & There

please take it
don't mend it
it's still missing
part of you
you permeate
here and there

Tears Of Nowhere

I break myself into million pieces
Then I reconstruct and break again.
Nowhere can I go, nothing can I do,
Do I feel numb or detached from you.
The left eye sheds, the right swallows;
It is just too close to tears, do hold back.
I dare not make a sound to break
The silence of the night, I'm no stranger.
I drop one little tear upon my cowardice,
Finding it helpful in forgiving sins.
It trickles down the cheeks with a sigh;
I cry myself to sleep and I tell myself:
'Better save my tears for another night;
Before I fall apart, I want to fall asleep.

Toss & Turn

I need to be repaired
Slowly, carefully, and wholly
The long nights, for the mumble
The wet pillows, for the rumble
It is not easy to tear the tears
And restore them in the eyes
It is not easy to fear the fear
And break the silence restlessly
How can I normalise the abnormal
Inside every part of me in disguise
I toss and I show myself the loss
I turn and finally I come to learn
I need not be repaired
In the midst of darkness
Is when I need you the most

Falling Steps

You take another step
Straight and blunt
Slowly you walk
Softly you whisper

You stride another step
Course the fatal edge
Gently you crawl
Badly you grab

You tread another step
Fall from the border
Silently you cry
Firmly I hold

The Forlorn Cold

The delicate seconds
  The sluggish minutes
    And the frosty hours
      Bring your fragrant years
      In front of my subtle face

      The shadowy perfumes
      Prompt me with silence
      Under the idle moon
      While hearing the bell
    I wake up in the cold again

The Lone Air

I want to borrow your kiss
When the autumn wind blows
And find me trembling with cold

I mimic a looming caress
Wiping my tears with rustling leaves
My face is tinged with reddish hue

I look no further
But the moonlight shelter
You are merely a nip in the air

The End

all the efforts we paid
all the secrets we told
all the moments we shared

beget the mess we made
build the pains we bore
bring down the love we loved

in the name of love in the name of love in the name of love

in the name of love in the name of love in the name of love in the name of love

in the name of love in the name of love in the name of love in the name of love in the name of love in the name of love in the name of love in the name of love in the name of love in the name of love in the name of love in

IN THE NAME of love IN THE NAME of love IN THE NAME of love IN THE NAME of love IN THE NAME of love

MANIA EROS PRAGMA MANIA EROS PRAGMA MANIA EROS PRAGMA MANI A EROS PRAGMA MANIA ERO S PRAGMA MANI A EROS PRAGMA

in the name of love in the name of love in the name of love in the name of love in the name of love in the name of love in the name of love in the name of love in the name of love in the name of love in the name of love in the name of love in the name of love in the name of love in

name of love in the name of love in the name of love in the name of love in the name of love in the name of love in the name of love in the name of love in the name of love in the name of love in the name of love in the name of love in the na me of love in the name of love in the name of love in the na

THE MIDDLE NAME :

Once

Once you said so
You did say so
Did never let go

Fragrance

Your odour comes to me like
A bottle of fragrance: edible
Like seeds, like flowers,
Which bloom in my early spring.
Your touchable butterflies
Soar above my nerves:
You sing me a lullaby
Craving at the heart of my prime.

I Think Of You

I think of you like a fierce fray,
Running my nerves a neon ray;
I think of you like an endless cave,
Echoes' howling sounding safe;
I think of you like a tempting dude,
Showing my soul a splendid nude;
I think of you like a weary Jude,
Escaping from a sinful hood;
I think of you like a crazy nut,
Waver to shiver I find no guts.

Morning Blue

With the warmth peeping through,
Love me slowly on a morning blue.
Your feverish solitude melts down to earth,
Cursing that what a morning of birth.

I crave for your name a hard dose,
To the moon and back in the midst of a rose.
Drenching in a sea of Monday blue,
The deathlike tranquility lies in you.

Insomnia

The moon reflects the silhouette of your face,
it begs me to think more of your tempting eyes.
When I robe myself under the moonlight,
I fall into the temperament with a sharp relief.
I want to keep this secret to myself; yet,
the darkness reveals my hidden cravings.
I exhale your name into the air, casting a shadow
of your innocent love bites on my window. Too
overwhelming to me, your mere pretence. It's your
happiness which makes it bitter. After all, you know
the concealed thought of me. I look at our unparalleled
photo, moaning about my insomnia.

Rain

It doesn't matter if it rains
As long as you dance
With me in the mushy rain

Longing For

I long for the night
When you whisper
To me marrowy soft.

I long for the night
When you touch me
Like a soulful queen.

I long for the night
When you behold me
Like a fateful duet.

I long for the night
As I can only feel
You in my dreams.

The East & The West

The rose wine tempts me in a mist
On a summer beach in late July.
The nature keeps you spinning
On the other side of the Asian East.

The silver lining lies on the shore
With your face caught in the horizon,
And when the sun asserts itself
In the surface of the Adriatic Sea.

Our shores and oceans will never meet
Under the sunny rain and the high tide,
Yet our hearts bring us together from
The East to the West during the sunset.

Kotor Heart

I long to see your kingdom
On the rugged mountains
Along the skirting black coast.

The crooked roads wickedly
Divide our territories into parts
Where independence declares.

The history of your Gulf of Kotor
Separates mountains and seas
Which people can never reach.

Road Trip

You rest beside me
With your tender
Eyelids half closed.

You sit in the shadow
Of the side window
Against the sunshine.

I drive all the way
Trying not to disturb
Your majestic breath.

I steal glances at you
From the late sunrise
Until the night grows.

The Blood Moon

I look up to the sky,
You are the one and
Only I can ever see.

Rarely is your red
With alluring shot,
Scantily irresistible.

You are at times
So far yet so close
For me to touch.

Lucky are the stars
Which recline on your
Adoringly elegance.

More Than December

There's something special in December
When babies are hugging their mother
And couples are kissing one another

There's something special in December
When you and I never reach each other
And I miss all those words I try to utter

Fill Me

Fill me with happiness
In the way I feel loved
Until the wound is healed
And the love is sealed.

The Ferris Wheel

Sitting on the rotating upright wheel,
We find ourselves swept downwards and upwards.
I look at your tender eyes which
Tell me a fanciful story of a berry farm.
The August essence blows into our cabin
And I tap on your shoulder for a fictive kiss.
You are too unreal for me to ask for that
So I turn and look down at the wan Church.
I use a second to remember that moment
And my heart beats too fast which scares my soul.
That is the first and last time we spend
On a Ferris wheel, and no more in a lifetime
Like that which goes so obsessed yet alluring.

Give You Poetry

You give me poetry when you
Sip the rim of my pink champagne.
You press your lips on my glass
And I find chaos and butterflies
Inside my chest and stomach.

Stirrings as my brains and nerves
Suddenly dazzle and excite that
I want to know more of you.
I take a liking to you and bring
You to the universe of uncertainty.

You fiddle with your hair, and when
Our eyes meet, your innocence
Hurries me to take control of your
Everything, to the moon and back.
And now, I want to give you poetry.

So Poetry

You are so poetry
Touching the silence
Seizing the dalliance
Gripping yet tearless
Longing yet callous
Off and on
You are more than poetry
With all these literary memories

Right

Love makes one right
But that
You make love right

The Wrong Hug

My nimble hands got paralysed
My warm hands froze
The way you made me quiver
When my arms were around you

Mosaic

I am a part of your heart
Which beats for your loneliness

I am a part of your lips
Which kiss for your scars

I am a part of your eyes
Which see the beauty in you

I am a part of your nerves
Which feel your secret pain

I am a special part of you
Who assemble to make you complete

Perfect Pitch

You don't sing well
But
You get the perfect pitch
Whenever
You call my name

Rain.
longing For
The We

Breath

I breathe in
Bits of you
Down the skin
You flow through

More & More

You say
the feelings are
more than words
I say
the words are
more than you

Lost

I know I'm
Lost with you
Carelessly
Faithfully
Crazily

A Crying Shadow

I breathed in the nightfall
Your silence cast a pall
Over the music once and for all

I had that summer in mind
When all were simply mine
Before you left me behind

The song played our story
The rhythm wrote its glory
Finding the memories hoary

I looked out of the window
In the glass I saw a crying shadow
Maybe it was too cold to snow

Under The Shade

I want to make you a morning coffee
Though I can't be your girl-to-be
You sit straight in front of me
But I'm too shy I just look at my knee
I understand in full your preference
As I take your everything as reference
You look cool when you walk past me
With your afternoon earl grey tea
Our eyes sometimes carelessly meet
And my heart starts a thousand beats
I envy those who befriend you
Always will I interrupt that's so true
It seems like you will not notice me
Being so dark and listless for you to see
But it's fine for me to continue to pray
For I enjoy staying under the shade

Secretly In Love

The shadows sway in my eyes;
I look at the nothingness in the photos
And holes and cuts and those goodbyes.
I gave you the ride that winter
When the air was still in the mist
And the music was whispered at your lips.
I turned to you that evening as I reckoned;
You counted the loneliness of the day
I counted the wrong timings in our way.
The rain did reveal your blues.
You were so tired that you were lost.
Sometimes all you needed was to laugh at
How silly I was to have loved you in this way
When you did not know much about me.
The melody in my car reminded me of
That evening when we spoke of romance.
At this moment I am quite sure
You do not remember that song
I played to reminisce the love story
Making up by me every morning.
And that's not the love I am longing.

A Love Letter

This is a love letter
For I know you will not read it
For I know how to stay alone
Under the snow and the tree

This is not a love letter
For I know you do not notice
For I know how to write it
With the sender name erased

No one will ever write a love letter
When the love is not known
When the writer does not send it
And you whom I love will just seal it

Good Night

You scream bits of tension at 5 a.m.
Thinking aloud out of nothing at all
For dusty thoughts get you broken
And insult the tranquility of the night
You do want to find a way back into love
I will fill you with dozens of poetry
Putting starlit words into your dreams
Wiping your fears, emptying your tears
Holding you tight and wishing you good night

Drug

Pondering over day and night
Toxic yet luscious and tempting
In which the heart consumes
I inhale
I ingest
I absorb
In the skin
Into the blood
Into every nerve and spine
The aftertaste stays
Sucking under my tongue
Lingering in memories
Until my saliva dissolves
In yours and many more
You cure my needs
My addiction and mood
You regulate my body heat
Should I discipline the dose
When I cannot control
It's more than irrational
I still
Crave for it and
Relish each moment
No matter how turbulent
You are

Upside Down

your hug
          seduces
violently
          like a squall
and a rainstorm
I still want
          to hold it
                    tight
until my world turns
          upside down

Quit

Your cult
Makes me sink
Makes me shrink
I promise to
Wear you off

I relapse again
Forthwith, submissively
When you are too
Alluring for me
To quit

Press Against

If you were the rain
I would be the rooftop

Please hit on me as hard as you can
Like how your lips press against mine

Kisses

Your kiss starts
a thunderstorm in my heart
It pierces through my back
and to my heart again
Back and forth
To and fro
Repeatedly
Until I am used to
the surge of it
Whenever I see you
I crave for
another thunder
another storm
Then I know
I am made for loving you
and I will not get enough
of all your irresistible kisses

Scent

I get caught up by your scent
The smell of your musk
Is so real and so true
It is almost intoxicating

When I'm near you
Your scent is too captivating
For me to taste and explore
I delve into your ears to your neck
Then your lips to your cheeks

When I leave you
Its uniqueness lingers
On my skin and fingertips
Scattering everywhere
Staying here and there

It is so strong that
I feel like you are inside of me
I feel so much about myself
That you are my integral piece

Touch

Phenomenal, it is phenomenal
To feel your touch at the arc
Of my shoulders in the dark
It truly heals and it sparks
Pondering where my secrets lie
They conquer all those goodbyes
And love needs not a prompt reply

Phenomenal, it is phenomenal
To run my fingers on your cheeks
I can hardly find words to speak
As your tenderness tastes so weak
Wondering where my secrets hide
They break into pieces and subside
When I feel so much about you inside

I can lose everything
But your touch

Blueprint

June is caught in the middle
Of the year, raining gently,
With the weight of cotton tree
Caressing your subtle face.
We are the twilight of universe,
Mirroring the distance of our
Journey; the summer sky drowns
Into the secrets of the golden sand,
Being buried, being forgotten.
With you by my side, your eyes
Speak of love and tenderness,
And this is my most yearning yet
Simple blueprint for my cryptic life.

Linger

Whenever I see you
I fall in love again
Let days be the same
Lingering at your name

Will You

(Verse I)

Will you send me flowers
When everyone tramples on them,
And guide me back into your root

Will you take my heart
When everyone thrusts at my chest,
And bring me back into the light

Will you embrace my weaknesses
When everyone curses me,
And take me back into quiet nights

Will You

(Verse II)

Will you still undress your soul
When suffering haunts you
In all the fragile conversations with me

Will you still paint a starry night
When melancholia dwells you
In all those shameful nights with me

Will you still dream a dream
When hopelessness fills you
In all the naked guilts confessed with me

Will You

(Verse III)

Will you
Collapse
Crack
Cry
Urge

If I
Swallow a sickle
Slash a vein
Scorch a bone
If I
Leave myself and
Walk away from you

The Manifest

The laughter belies
Her piercing grief.
In times of guilt
She gives her everything
And counts every touch.
With gusto
She believes in
Velvet nights
Holding someone
Tight, tautly, closely.
For another night and
For one more night
The pain dilutes
In someone's arms.
She keeps a secret
She cries a breath
She takes every
Solitary moment
In that maddening
Shout for love.
Better goodbyes
She still lies and hides.

The Figment

In a storm of tears
I squeezed my way through the crowd
To arrive at the station in good time

In a sea of people
I sought to find an intimate face
To dwindle my longing in an unfamiliar city

In a tunnel of darkness
I heard nothing but the echoes of my voice
To murmur your name in the distant cries

In a sally of attempts
I cannot reach you at this very moment just
To find myself spinning my wheels in here

The Haunting Night

I speak like smoked ashes
wanting to cry and pray
with my knees on carpet
I stay still and feel
the night I whisper
the night I struggle
I stay alone again
I am shattered, like...
a wave of nostalgia
leaving me behind
I shake a voice, quivering
trying to find a missing
piece of haunted soul
that can fit into a night
like this, like how lonely
it can be
nothing else but
it is

A Lifetime A Day

I have walked a lifetime with you
In every single day
From sun sets till night falls
For all four seasons begin
From rain pours till snow falls
Going through thick and thin

We have lived a life together
In every single day
For we love each other
Like it is the last that we have
And live as one as we do
With each moment as true as we two

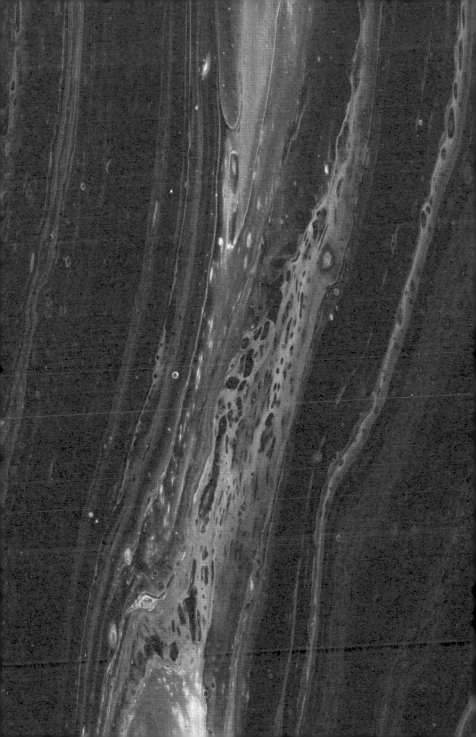

III

THE LAST NAME :
PRAGMA

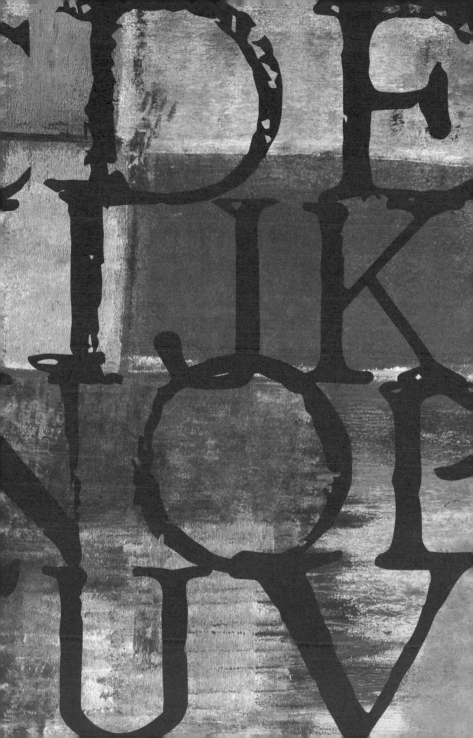

// YOU ARE THE REASON
I WRITE //

I write vigorously
Because you exist
Sometimes I become
Illiterate when
You walk away
I will keep writing
Until my body and
Soul are a part of
The prose and verse
I write for you
You are the reason I
Write
When there is nothing
Right

// YOU ARE THE REASON I FALL //

All In Or Nothing

I'm all in for you
And nothing for me

I have lost all of me
To love all of you
I have risked all of me
To hold all of you

All in or nothing
It's worth everything

// YOU ARE THE REASON
I AWAIT //

We bath ourselves
In the sunlight
And look golden
When the ray
Shoots our shadows
On the mountain

We robe ourselves
In the moonlight
And look silver
When the ray
Casts our shades
On the sea

We are awaiting
Our subway to
Lead our way
When the magic hour
Grabs the uncertainties
To our faraway future

// YOU ARE THE REASON
I DARE //

I wish to the day and I pray
I can expose myself to the light
And not to be kept in the dark
I take the courage of our conviction
Together we risk it all and take the fall
We keep our heads above the water
Surviving through the dreamy flaw
Becoming an audacious one to all
In the face of doubt you show bravery
We kiss the scars and look at the stars
I wish to one day and I pray
Holding hands we awake at the first light
Looking at your eyes within my sight
With you travelling through the age of time
Bestowing the meaning of life in our prime

// YOU ARE THE REASON I GLITTER //

Give You A Sunset

Your eyes ray out a sunset
Beaming with savoury delight
I reserve all the sun rays
And put them in a jar of love
I find sun shower in your glamour
It rotates round the horizon
Then to your waist and back
Our flame is still striking
From twilight into the dusk
I draw a full circle in your lips
Down to the surface and up again
Somehow and sometimes
I keep looking at the glitters
That I have missed the sunset
Yet I will spend my whole lifetime
To give you a thousand sunsets

// YOU ARE THE REASON I CHERISH //

I'm afraid there isn't enough time
To share with you the fragrance of life
I'm afraid there isn't enough time
To show you the allure of day and night
Whenever you smile and mime
Whispering "save it for next time"

// YOU ARE THE REASON I RISE //

I was bent
in the expectations of others
I was shot
in the gulf of warlike life
I was spurned
in the evil of the tongues
I was mistaken
in the remedy of the soul
I was dumped
in the breath of sinfulness

Hitherto
I am not broken
when I see you

// YOU ARE THE REASON
I DROWN //

You are the tide and knots and
An integral part of the vast ocean
Attaching to the emergence of life
Encircling my whole unmapped world
That cannot be trapped and scrapped

The bluish colour is so distinct that
Your unknown visible glow comes to life
I indulge in your deluge of circulation
Witnessing your agitation in calmness
And I go mad about your cave and waves

Little do I know your breadth and depth
But I will get drunk and sunk in this spiral
Until I have explored the unexplored
Until I have breathed out the last breath
Until I am drenched and drowned in you

// YOU ARE THE REASON
I SEEK //

I will send you flowers and amend your scars
I will sing you a song by the shore playing my guitar
In another life I will elope with you in a car and just go far

In another life grant me the might to stay by your side
I will store the sunlight and anchor it by your bedside
I will take pride for love was needless to hide

I will cross the sky and find you amongst the stars
I will move the mountain lift the sea and live without a mar
In another life I will stay where I am and meet you from afar

In this life I will hold you tight if there is no tomorrow
I will walk following your shadow and keep pace slow
I will love you more and find you once again in another life I know

I WILL KNOW YOU
ONCE AGAIN

I will know you once again in my lifetime
When the emergent feelings set in
When I can't control my arms
When my heartbeat can't last any longer
Though I can't hold you right now
I will know you once again
I'm sure

TIMING KNOWS NO LOVE

Timing knows no love
for someone crawls in my thought

It doesn't take us long to perch
the minute and second hands
on every single sip of wine we drink
and on every gentle blow we make.

Timing knows no love
on days and nights like this.

It takes us an hour or a lifetime
to create our own period
which is forever meant for you
and together we get withered

until timing knows a love
which links our names for all time.

KEEP WAITING

By no means, waiting in haste,
waiting in silence, long enough
for the rest of our life waiting,
as the clock keeps the world spinning.
It is not long enough to extend in space
or time to wait for a company like this.
Our love is clocked by the palm,
by silence, by the tears, by the distance
that cannot be counted or calculated.
To measure a life with your name in the
edge of doom, to measure a love that
cannot be measured, evermore, on and on,
is a gesture under the harvest moon.
I keep you waiting, for life, by all means.

DON'T WANT YOU
TO SEE ME WEEP

Don't want you to see me weep
When I am weak staying in bed
You still have promises to keep
Before I dash to the future ahead
And forget about you in my head

Don't want you to see me weep
When I am anguished and in pain
Just find peace when you fall asleep
Learn to dance and sing in the rain
Though all blood and sweat are in vain

Don't want you to see me weep
When I softly call out your name
Let me wipe the tears you seep
It must be a fame to be your dame
And on my grave carving your last name

IN THE ENDS
OF THE EARTH

I will be yours
and I am yours
devoutly
f anatically
like the flowers
in the bloom of love

LEI KA MAN CARMEN IS A POET, ARTIST, AND EDUCATOR. SHE IS A PASSIONATE TEACHER WHO ENJOYS DOING MANY THINGS. REALLY. MANY.

Carmen
Lei

CARMEN IS CURRENTLY A PART-TIME UNIVERSITY LECTURER AND A FULL-TIME ENGLISH TEACHER IN A MIDDLE SCHOOL. SHE IS THE JUNIOR SECONDARY ENGLISH PANEL CHAIRPERSON, THE COORDINATOR OF THE ACADEMIC DEVELOPMENT TEAM, A MEMBER OF THE PROFESSIONAL DEVELOPMENT TEAM, AND A CLASS TEACHER. BESIDES ACADEMIC, SHE IS THE ADVISER OF THE ST. MAGDALENE SOCIAL WORK CLUB. SHE IS RESPONSIBLE FOR THE VOLUNTARY WORK AND CHARITABLE EVENTS OF THE SCHOOL. SHE LED AND ENCOURAGED STUDENTS TO CREATE NEARLY 100 POEMS, WHICH WERE COMPILED AND PUBLISHED INTO A COLLECTION OF POEMS CALLED "THE SOUND OF WORDS". OUTSIDE THE SCHOOL, SHE IS AN ACTIVE MEMBER OF THE COMMUNITY. SHE IS THE MANAGING DIRECTOR OF THE MACAO ASSOCIATION FOR THE ADVANCEMENT OF ENGLISH LANGUAGE TEACHING, THE MANAGING DIRECTOR OF THE MACAO ASSOCIATION OF TEACHER VOLUNTEERS, AND THE SECRETARY GENERAL OF MACAU ASSOCIATION FOR THE ADVANCEMENT OF DIVERSIFIED DEVELOPMENT.

ABOUT THE AUTHOR

CARMEN LIKES TO USE UP EVERY SECOND. WHEN SHE'S NOT SLEEPING.
YOU MAY FIND HER

DRINKING

DOING SPORTS

HANGING OUT

WRITING

DRAWING

READING

TUTORING

LECTURING

THINKING

CARMEN'S POETRY AND PROSE EXPLORES THE MANY FACETS OF LOVE AND
RELATIONSHIPS.

OBSESSION

POSSESSION

BETRAYAL

LOSS

HEALING

LITERALLY. THIS IS A COLLECTION OF HER MESSY SECRETS.

BOOK TITLE: IN THE NAME OF LOVE

AUTHOR: LEI KA MAN, CARMEN
PROOFREAD BY: WONG UN FONG

DESIGNED BY: BENNY TANG POU I
PRINTED BY: MUSE-UM. CO

FIRST PUBLISHED: JUNE 2022

PUBLISHED BY: MACAO TYPE DESIGN SOCIETY
DISTRIBUTED BY: MACAOGRAPHY

SUGGESTED PRICE: MOP 180.00

SUBJECTS: POETRY, LITERATURE, ART

ISBN 978-99981-836-4-3

ISBN 978-99981-836-4-3

9 789998 183643

THE TYPEFACE
TYPOGRAPHER - BENNY TANG POU I

OBRAS 1940

T

THE SAN SERIF FONT FIRST CAME FROM A STONE TABLET OF 1940 IN
THE LEAL SENADO. THIS FONT HAS SIMPLE LINES. THICK STROKES. AND
IS ALL IN UPPER CASE. THE CROSSBAR POSITIONS OF THE LETTERS
A. E. AND F ARE VERY SPECIAL. THE OVERALL LETTERS ARE QUITE
NARROW IN SIZE . I STARTED SUPPLEMENTING THE CHARACTERS
(GLYPHS) IN 2018.

FONTS USED IN THE 2ND CHAPTER: MERCY ENGLISH ROUNDHAND

T

THIS ENGLISH ROUNDHAND DRAWS FROM THE ORIGINAL MANUSCRIPT
ON THE FIRST PAGE OF THE STATUES (COMMITMENT) OF THE MACAU
HOLY HOUSE OF MERCY. WRITTEN IN 1662 AFTER ITS DRAFTING
AND APPROVAL IN 1667. IT IS THE OLDEST HISTORICAL DOCUMENT
PRESERVED BY THE MACAU HOLY HOUSE OF MERCY.
I HAD TO DO REPAIR AND RESTORATION (EXPANSION OF THE FONTS)
WORKS. INCLUDING PRECISION CORRECTION OF THE LINES BETWEEN THE
LETTERS. AND A LOT OF KERNING AND FINE-TUNINGS.

FONTS USED IN THE 3RD CHAPTER

T

I TOOK A LOT OF LETTERS FROM THE BOOK *CHRISTIANI PUERI
INSTITUTIO.* RANDOMLY ASSIGNED CODES TO THEM AND THEN ASSEMBLED
THE CODED LETTERS INTO MULTIPLE CHARACTER SETS. THUS ALLOWING
EACH POEM IN THIS CHAPTER TO PRESENT DIFFERENT FONT STYLES.
CHRISTIANI PUERI INSTITUTIO IS THE FIRST LATIN BOOK IN CHINA.
PRINTED IN 1588 IN MACAO BY CATHOLIC PRIESTS USING LEAD
MOVABLE TYPEFACE. TODAY. WITH DIGITAL TYPEFACE TECHNOLOGY.
THE LATIN TYPEFACE IS BROUGHT BACK TO US FROM THE OLD MACAO
MORE THAN 430 YEARS AGO.

LET

MY

LOVE

BE

HEARD